AIRPORT

PHILIP SAUVAIN

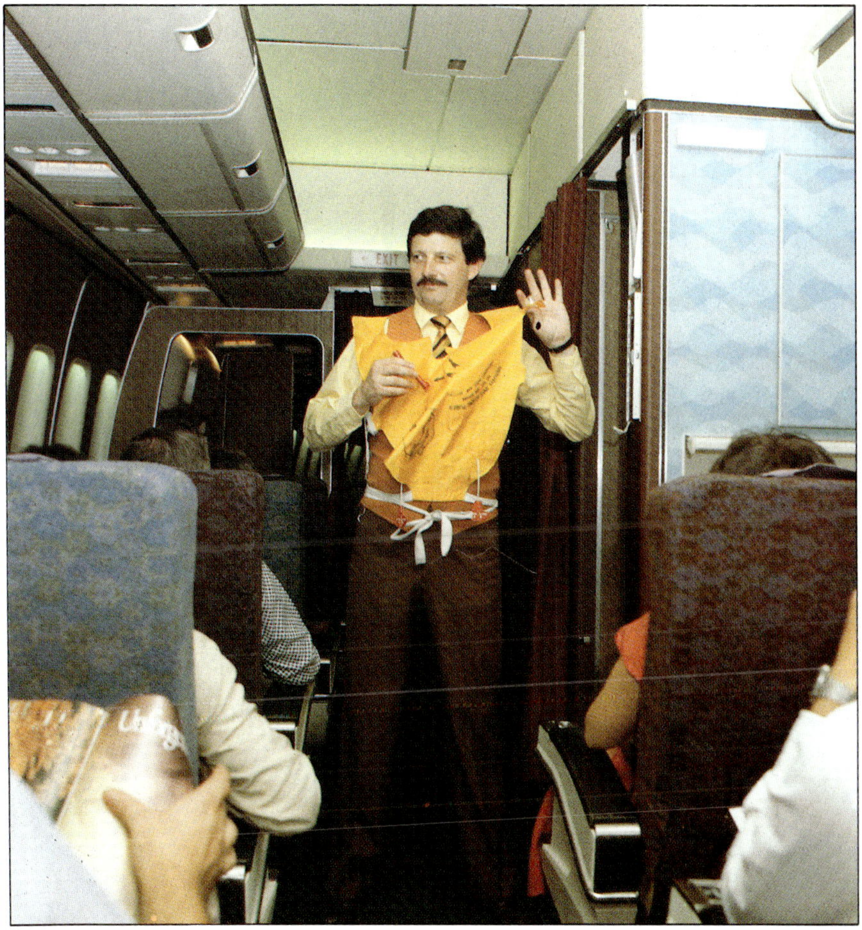

Editorial planning
Philip Steele

SILVER BURDETT PRESS

Copyright © 1988 by Schoolhouse Press, Inc.
an imprint of Silver Burdett Inc.
Prentice Hall Building, Route 9W,
Englewood Cliffs, N.J. 07632

Original copyright, © Macmillan Education Limited 1988
© BLA Publishing Limited 1988

Designed and produced by BLA Publishing Limited,
East Grinstead, Sussex, England.

A Ling Kee Company

Illustrations by Steve Lings/Linden Artists and Sebastian
Quigley/Linden Artists
Printed in Hong Kong

88/89/90/91/92/93   6 5 4 3 2 1

Library of Congress Cataloging-in-Publication Data

Sauvain, Philip Arthur.
  In an airport.
  (The World of work)
  Includes index.
  Summary: Describes the history, services, personnel, and
daily activities of airports.
  1. Airports — Juvenile literature. [1. Airports.] I. Title.
II. series.

TL725.S37   1988
387.7'36 — dc 19

ISBN 0-382-09721-1

Photographic credits

t = top b = bottom l = left r = right

cover: British Caledonian

4, 5t, 5b ZEFA; 6t BBC Hulton Picture Library;
6b Aviation Picture Library; 7 Quadrant Picture Library;
8, 9 ZEFA; 10t British Airports Authority; 10b, 11
British Caledonian; 14 J. Allan Cash; 15t ZEFA;
15b Aviation Picture Library; 16t British Airports
Authority; 16b ZEFA; 17 Aviation Picture Library;
18 Chris Fairclough Picture Library; 19t ZEFA;
19b Barnaby's Picture Library; 20 ZEFA; 21t British
Airports Authority; 21b, 22, 23t Aviation Picture
Library; 23b British Caledonian; 24 Barnaby's Picture
Library; 26 British Airports Authority; 27t, 27b Aviation
Picture Library; 28 British Caledonian; 29 British Airports
Authority; 30 ZEFA; 31t J. Allan Cash; 31b ZEFA;
32 British Airports Authority; 33t British Caledonian;
33b Chris Fairclough Picture Library; 34 ZEFA;
35 J. Allan Cash; 36 ZEFA; 37t, 37b, 38 Chris Fairclough
Picture Library; 39t, 39b ZEFA; 40 J. Allan Cash;
41t British Caledonian; 41b Chris Fairclough Picture
Library; 42, 43 ZEFA

How To Use This Book:
This book has many useful features. For example, look at the table of contents. See how it describes
each section in the book. Find a section you want to read and turn to it.

Notice that the section is a "two-page spread." That is, it covers two facing pages. Now look at
the headings in the spread. Headings are useful when you want to locate specific information. Next,
look at a photograph, drawing, chart or map and find its caption. Captions give you additional
information. A chart or map may also have labels to help you.

Scan the spread for a word in **bold print**. If you cannot find one in this spread, find one in
another spread. Bold-print words are defined in the glossary at the end of the book. Find your
bold-print word in the glossary.

Now turn to the index at the end of the book. When you have a specific topic or subject to
research, look for it in the index. you will quickly know whether the topic is in the book.

We hope you will use the features in this book to help you learn about new and exciting things.

Contents

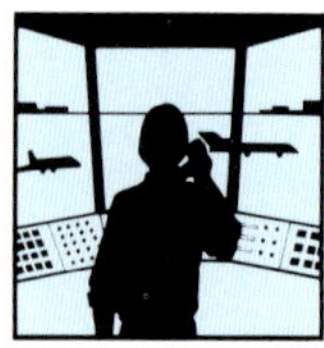

Introduction

▼ At busy airports with several runways, planes take off and land at the rate of more than one a minute. At these large airports many thousands of people are employed to take care of passengers and cargo.

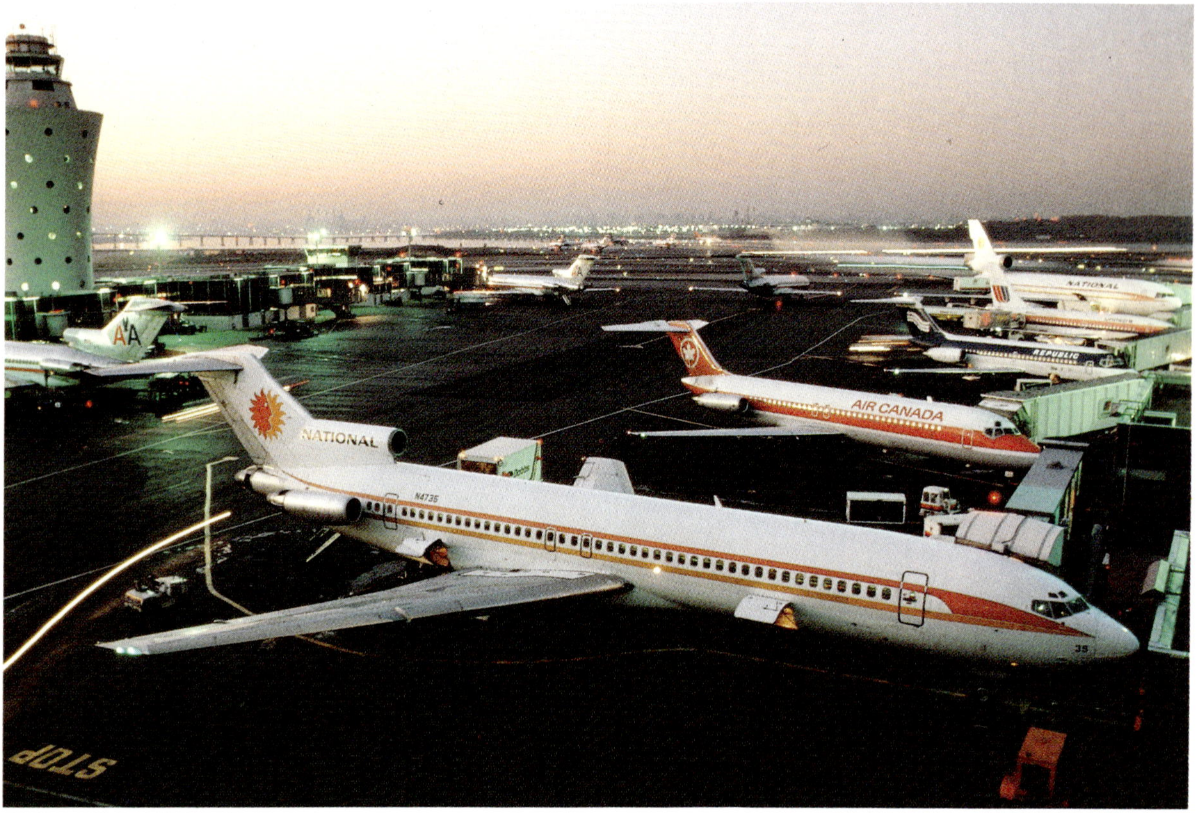

In Alice Springs, Australia, a small plane takes off to pick up a little girl who has broken a leg, and carry her to the nearest hospital. In Topeka, Kansas, a farmer loads his plane with crop-spraying equipment. A plane drops food and medical supplies for the drought victims in Ethiopia. The Schmidt family boards a plane at Frankfurt Airport in Germany for their summer vacation in the sun.

People travel by plane all over the world today. Air travel has become one of the most important means of transportation. Most people fly in **airliners**. Airliners are the large planes which are owned and run by companies called **airlines**. Airliners do not carry passengers only. They also carry **cargo**, such as newspapers, medicines, mail, and machinery.

A Place to Land

All planes need clear areas of land or water on which to land and take off, called runways. Small planes can use a short runway, such as a grass field or even a sandy beach. Large airliners need a long runway with a smooth, hard surface.

The airliners carry several hundred people at a time, and many thousands of people are employed by airlines all over the world to take care of the passengers and cargo.

Working at an Airport

In a large international airport, thousands of people work in the offices, workshops, restaurants, and shops. They all help to make sure that the airport runs smoothly.

Every day, many flights leave for airports in other countries. Planes also fly **domestic flights**, or journeys within the same country. All these flights are controlled from a tall building at the center of the airport called the **control tower**. This is where the **air traffic controllers** work. They organize the movement of the planes in the sky and on the ground.

▼ Passengers arriving at Frankfurt Airport in Germany.

▼ Keeping the arrivals and departures board correct and up to date is just one of the many jobs to be done by the airport staff.

The First Airports

On December 17, 1903, at Kitty Hawk North Carolina, Orville Wright took off into the air in Flyer 1. He flew for twelve seconds and traveled a distance of 120 feet. Orville and his brother Wilbur were the first people to fly a plane. Their success changed the world.

In 1909, Louis Blériot flew from France to England. This was the first time anyone had flown from one country to another. The first person to cross the Atlantic Ocean in a plane without stopping was the American, Charles Lindbergh. He took off from New York on May 20, 1927 and arrived in Paris thirty-three hours later. The courage of these pioneers of flight helped to make low cost air travel possible.

▲ A passenger plane flies over the tea-garden and restaurant at Templehof Airport in Germany in the 1920s. There were very few facilities for the passengers while they waited for their flight.

◀ The job of an airline pilot in the 1930s was very different from that of an airline pilot today. To avoid bad weather over the English Channel, British pilots often crossed it no more than forty feet above the sea!

▲ Idlewild Airport in the United States in 1955. With increased air travel in the 1950s, airports began to employ more people and put up better buildings to deal with passengers and cargo.

The First Airliners

The early airliners were very different from the huge Boeing 747s, or **jumbo jets**, of today. The early planes of the 1920s carried only ten to twenty passengers, unlike the jumbo jet which can carry between 350 and 500 passengers. In the 1920s, airliners often began to carry letters and parcels as well as passengers. This was the beginning of **airmail**.

In those days, flying was risky. The flights were bumpy because of the weather at lower levels. The passengers were often airsick. The runways were much shorter than those of today, and takeoffs and landings were often dangerous.

The pilots of the early airliners not only had to fly the planes, but also had to load the baggage and often had to repair the planes, too. On flights from London to Paris, the pilots carried chewing gum in case it was needed to stop leaks!

The first airliners had few comforts. There were no flight attendants to serve meals or drinks. The journeys were long, slow, and cold. The pilots also had to land frequently to refuel.

Early Airports

Because the first airliners were small and carried few passengers, they were also expensive to run. Yet, despite the high cost of air travel, there were few comforts for the passengers before or after takeoff. Airports were very simple. Many were just fields where the passengers waited in wooden buildings or even in tents. Only a few airports had buildings made of brick or concrete.

The Age of Flight

By the 1950s, air travel was becoming more popular. In 1945, jet engines had come into use, and the first jet airliner appeared in 1949. This meant that air travel was faster. When the jumbo jet was introduced in 1969, air travel also became cheaper because so many more people could be carried on one flight. This growth in air travel meant that more people were needed to work for the airlines.

Around the World

Today, there are airports all over the world and in all kinds of places. Some are in remote areas, like the airport at Lhasa in Tibet which is 14,180 feet up in the Himalayan Mountains. Some, such as the Pacific island of Tonga, are so tiny that very good navigation is needed to find them.

Other airports cover vast areas, like King Khalid International Airport at Riyadh in Saudi Arabia, which is the largest airport in the world. However, the world's busiest airport is Chicago's O'Hare International Airport.

Most of the passengers who land at O'Hare fly on to other parts of the United States using connecting flights. Nearly 55 million passengers travel in and out of this airport a year, and there is a takeoff and a landing every 39.66 seconds.

Where are Airports Located?

Airports have to be easy to travel to from nearby towns and cities. Also, fast, efficient transportation is needed to take passengers and cargo on to their final destination after they have landed. However, building an airport in or near a city can cause problems. The noise of jet airliners taking off and landing can disturb people who live nearby. Sometimes, the pilots have difficulty landing because of tall buildings. For example, landing in Hong Kong can be difficult because of the skyscrapers. As a result, many airports are built several miles away from the cities that they serve.

▼ A remote airport in the Hadramaut region of the People's Democratic Republic of Yemen. In this mountainous, desert region where travel is difficult, the plane can bring in much needed goods.

Flying Worldwide

There is no other means of transportation that needs as much international agreement as air travel. No one authority is in charge of all the airports and airlines in the world. However, there is great cooperation between the various people involved. Government representatives and airline officials from all over the world meet regularly. They agree on international safety measures, which airlines can fly where and on which routes, and also the fares the airlines should charge. They also enter into agreements about which countries' planes can enter the **airspace**, or the sky, above a particular country.

▲ The airport staff at Chicago's O'Hare Airport are kept busy making sure every plane is ready for takeoff.

▶ This map shows the journeys flown every month by the airliners of Japan Airlines. A similar map showing all the routes flown by all the world's airlines would look like a spider's web. The thickest part of the web would be over the United States.

Who Runs an Airport?

A large international airport is run by an **airport authority**. This authority either owns the airport or runs it on behalf of a government or a private firm. The airport authority employs thousands of people.

The Airport Management

The manager, or **administrator**, in charge of an airport has an important job. He or she has to make sure that everything works smoothly. An administrator is responsible for the choice of the airlines that use the airport. He or she has to act as the link between those airlines or anyone wishing to use the airport's facilities and the airport employees.

◄ Computers can be used by the staff at busy airports to book tickets, plan flights, and pay wages.

Larger airports may be divided into several **terminals,** and each one has its own manager. These managers look after the day-to-day business of the terminals. There are many problems that arise when a lot of people doing different jobs work in the same building. The terminal managers deal with the people who run the shops, banks, and restaurants in the airport.

The airport and terminal managers have to make sure that the airport's police, fire, and medical services can deal quickly with any emergency. There may be a fire. An airliner may lose a wheel and have to be towed off the runway. If there is a major accident, such as an air crash, the managers coordinate the airport's emergency services with any that may be needed from nearby towns or cities.

Airport Staff

Over 100,000 people pass through a large international airport in the course of a day. The airport staff has to be able to deal with such large numbers. They have to be trained to do their jobs under difficult conditions. Air traffic controllers, for example, may have to deal with hundreds of extra flights if bad weather has delayed the planes, or just before a national holiday.

▼ The flight operations manager has to keep an up to date record of each airliner's movements.

Inside the Airport

In large airports, terminals are either separated into departures and arrivals, or between the various airlines. Sometimes, they are divided according to areas of the world. In whichever way the terminals are organized, they are the scene of constant activity.

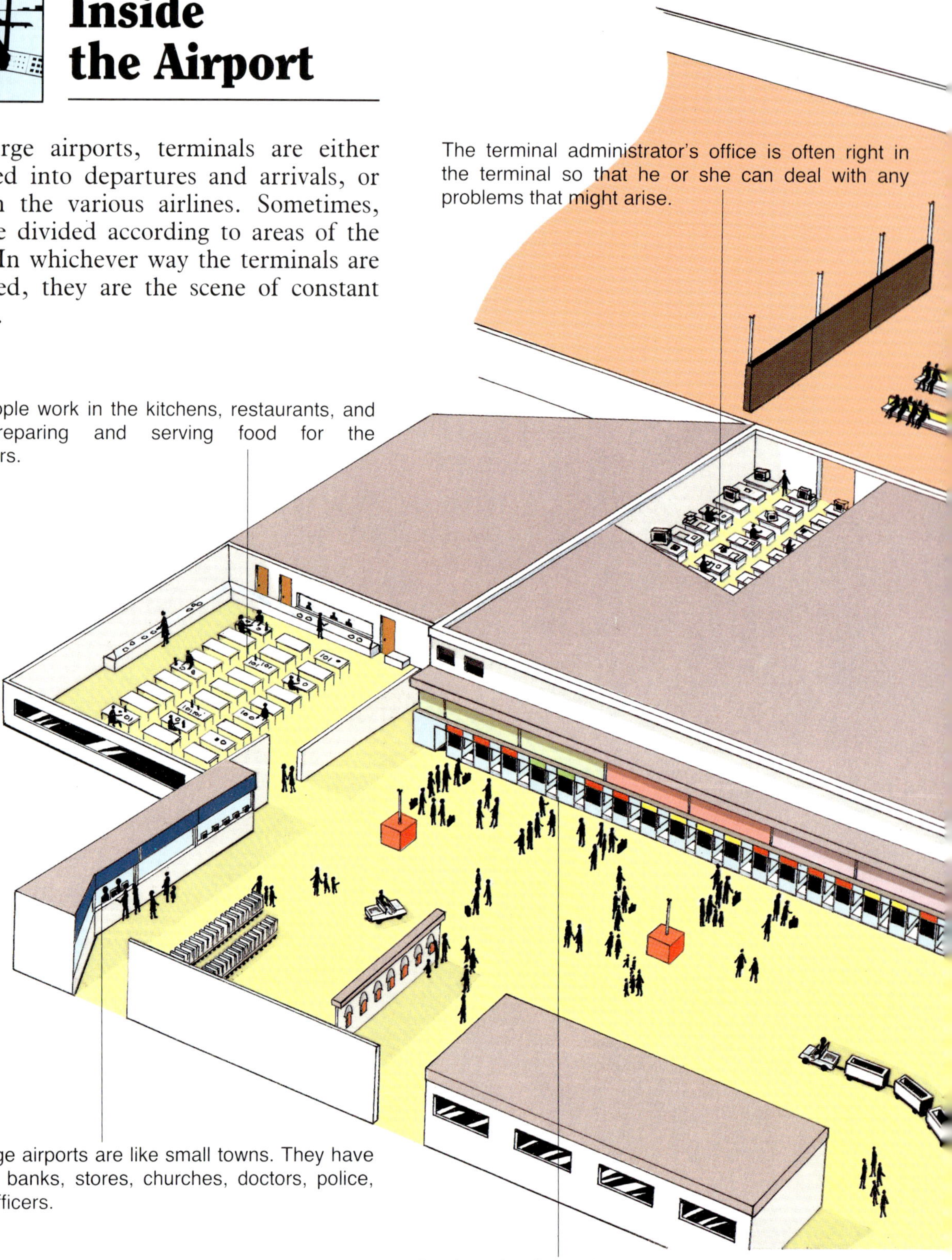

Many people work in the kitchens, restaurants, and cafés preparing and serving food for the passengers.

Some large airports are like small towns. They have their own banks, stores, churches, doctors, police, and fire officers.

The terminal administrator's office is often right in the terminal so that he or she can deal with any problems that might arise.

At the **check-in** desks, the airline staff checks passenger tickets and weighs their baggage.

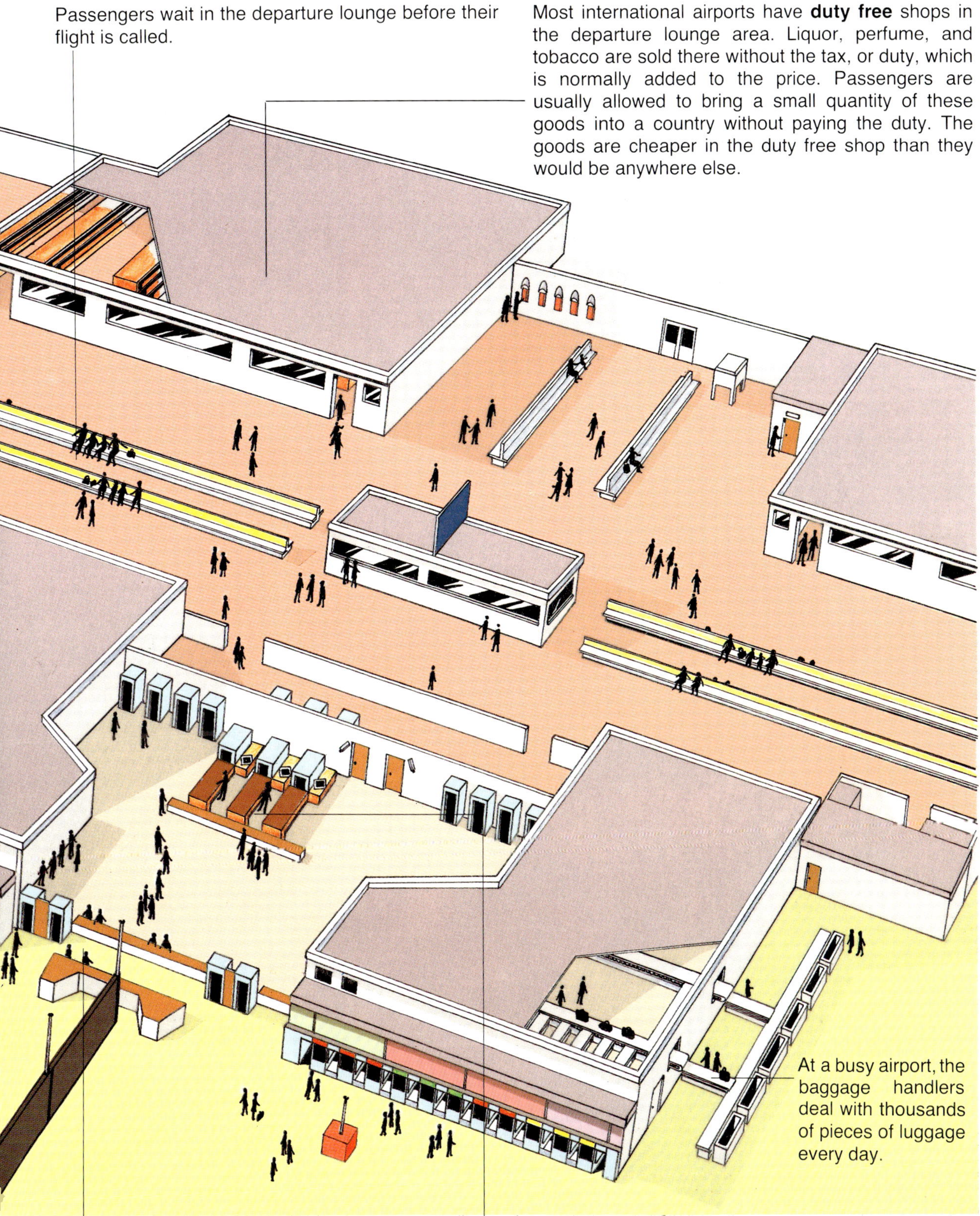

Passengers wait in the departure lounge before their flight is called.

Most international airports have **duty free** shops in the departure lounge area. Liquor, perfume, and tobacco are sold there without the tax, or duty, which is normally added to the price. Passengers are usually allowed to bring a small quantity of these goods into a country without paying the duty. The goods are cheaper in the duty free shop than they would be anywhere else.

At a busy airport, the baggage handlers deal with thousands of pieces of luggage every day.

As passengers pass through **customs**, their passports are checked by customs officers.

Security officers check the passengers and their hand baggage for dangerous objects. Their job is to protect the passengers and airline staff.

At the Terminal

The busiest part of the airport is the terminal building. This is filled with the hustle and bustle of travelers and their friends and families coming and going. Hundreds of workers are employed in the terminal building to serve the needs of the passengers.

Transportation Workers

The work of an airport begins outside the terminal building. Hundreds of transportation workers supply a service to passengers. These workers drive the buses, taxis, limousines, and trains that take the passengers to and from the airport.

Passengers are sometimes driven to the airport by friends or relatives, so most large airports have short-term parking lots. However, if passengers are going away for some time, perhaps on vacation, or on a business trip, they can leave their cars in long-term parking lots. These lots are managed by attendants who watch over the cars and collect the parking fees.

▼ Passengers use all forms of transportation to get to an airport. These cars are British taxis. Most airlines suggest that the passengers should check in at least one hour before takeoff.

▲ Passengers change their own money into the currency of the country to which they are flying at the airport bank.

Store Clerks

Inside the main hall and the departure lounge of the terminal building, many people work as clerks in stores, selling items like books, candy, or makeup that travelers may have forgotten or may need on the journey. Some clerks work in stores that sell souvenirs or even clothing.

Other Workers

The terminal also houses many other services for the passengers. Large airports will have cleaners, electricians, and plumbers to keep the airport facilities clean, neat, and working well. Sometimes, there is also a medical center with nurses and an airport doctor. Many airports have their own special police forces, too.

Restaurants, snack bars, and lounges also provide jobs for cooks, waiters and waitresses, cashiers, and bartenders.

▶ Many staff are employed by airports to work in restaurants and cafés.

The Check-in Desk

When passengers arrive at the terminal building, they go first to the check-in desk. There, a staffmember of the airline they are traveling with will check their tickets and baggage, and direct them to their flights.

Most passengers buy their tickets in advance at a travel agent's or from the airline itself. Some passengers arrive at the terminal without tickets, hoping that there will be some room left on a flight. This usually means that they can buy their tickets at a lower price.

Certain flights, called **shuttle flights**, run over short distances several times every day. For these flights, passengers buy a general ticket which they can use at any time, provided that they check in before the particular flight is full.

▲ Each airline has its own check-in desks and staff. Passengers present their tickets and check in their baggage.

▶ Every passenger must hand a boarding pass to the stewardess before they can board the plane.

The Check-in Staff

Members of the check-in staff dress in the uniform of the airline for which they work. They need to be well organized and patient. They may be faced with a long line of passengers, and with people who do not speak the local language. Some check-in staffmembers are trained in the use of computers which help them to do their job faster and more efficiently. It is possible for a member of the staff to deal with as many as a hundred passengers in an hour.

Checking the Ticket

A passenger hands over his or her ticket. The check-in staff member feeds the details into the airline's computer or checks them against a list of reservations that is kept on the computer.

If the ticket is in order, the staffmember then makes out a **boarding pass**, which shows that the passenger is cleared to board the plane. The staffmember writes a seat assignment number on it, and enters the seat number into the computer. Then, if the passenger has luggage, it is weighed and the weight is written on the ticket by the check-in staff. Because only a certain amount of weight can be carried by the plane, each passenger is allowed only a limited amount of baggage.

When it has been weighed, the check-in staffmember tags the baggage which shows the number of the flight and where it is going. A **conveyor belt** sends the baggage to the sorting room to be put on the right plane. The passenger keeps hand luggage, such as a handbag or a briefcase.

Handling Baggage

The airline employs a large number of baggage handlers to move baggage between the terminal and the planes and to load and unload the planes. In most large airliners, the baggage is stored in a space known as the **cargo hold** which runs underneath the passenger cabin.

Baggage Labels

Busy airports handle as many as 10,000 pieces of baggage in an hour. When the baggage reaches the sorting room, the baggage handlers look at the labels which tell them where the baggage is going. A flight number, such as AA 123 tells them the name of the airline, which is American Airlines, and that the number of the flight is 123. Three other letters on the label give the name of the airport to which it is going. For example, LHR means London Heathrow and MEL means Melbourne.

The Sorting Room

In the sorting room, a clerk checks the label and puts the baggage on another conveyor belt. When the sorting clerk presses a button, a machine tips the baggage off the conveyor belt into the right chute for that flight.

▼ Although much of the work of an airport can be done efficiently by machines and computers, it is difficult to handle baggage in the same way. Here, in the baggage sorting-room, the handlers make sure that each passenger's baggage will be loaded onto the right plane.

▲ At large airports, handlers use conveyor belts to load the baggage into the hold of the airliner.

Loading Up

Baggage handlers pile the baggage for each airliner on a small **baggage train**. A driver on a small tractor pulls the long line of these wagons onto the area in front of the terminal where the plane is waiting. Fork-lifts are often used to lift the baggage and load it into the cargo hold of the airliner.

Collecting Baggage

When the plane arrives at its destination, the baggage is unloaded. Baggage handlers transport it to the terminal where it is unloaded and put on to turntables called **carousels**. As the carousels go around, the passengers look for and then claim their baggage.

▶ Baggage is unloaded onto the carousel and it goes around and around until passengers remove it.

Security

Airlines and airport authorities across the world work to stop people from carrying guns, explosives, and other weapons onto a plane. This is to prevent anyone from taking over, or hijacking, the plane. Also, if a gun went off by accident, it might kill someone or cause the plane to crash.

Security officers are employed at the airport to protect the passengers and airline staff. It is their job to search all passengers and to inspect suitcases or other containers before they are loaded onto the plane.

Training

The security officers have to understand the way in which weapons or explosives work. If they find anything dangerous, they need to know how to handle it safely.

The officers are trained to recognize suspicious behaviour. They must be alert at all times and know everything that is happening at their airport. They must also be in touch with security officers at other airports. To do this, the security officers are trained to use computers. The work of a security officer is helped by reports about suspects sent in by the police.

▼ A security officer watches while passengers pass through the airport's metal detector.

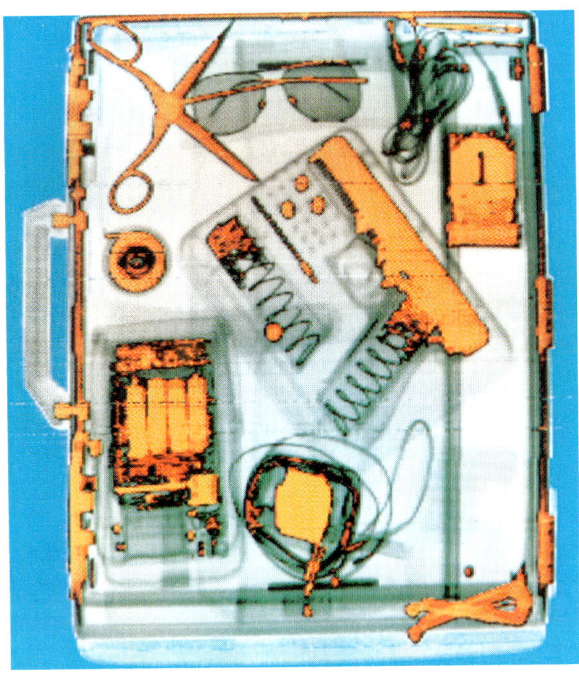

Checking Hand Baggage

Metal objects, such as guns, can be detected by the security officers in two ways. First, they search the passenger's hand baggage using an **X-ray machine**. This takes a picture with light rays that show what is inside someone's luggage. The shape of a gun or knife will show up on the screen even if it is hidden among clothes. Secondly, the passengers have to walk through a **metal detector**. This machine rings or buzzes if there is any metal object in the passengers' clothes. Sometimes the metal detector is set off by keys, jewelry, or belt buckles. The passenger removes whatever is making the machine go off and walks through it again. If the machine goes off again, the security officer will search the passenger.

▲ Security officers pay particular attention to regular flights to countries whose airliners have been attacked by terrorists in the past. Passengers could hide a gun or a knife in their baggage. Can you see the gun in this X-ray photograph?

▶ The luggage is put through a special X-ray machine on a conveyor belt. The officer examines the X-ray image for any dangerous objects.

Customs and Immigration

Whenever you visit a foreign country, you must carry a **passport**. This document contains your photograph and gives your name, country, place and date of birth, height, and any distinguishing marks. These details are checked by customs officers at the airport. They are trained to make sure that the photograph and details in your passport match your appearance.

Customs officers also check the passports of people returning from a foreign country. This is called **immigration control**. Some passengers may have to carry a special entry form called a **visa**. This allows them to stay in a country only for a specific length of time.

If a customs officer thinks a passenger is suspicious, he or she can feed the passport number into a computer. The number is checked to see if the passport is stolen or belongs to someone wanted by the police.

Baggage Check

Customs officers also check to see if passengers are carrying dangerous drugs or trying to smuggle in goods without paying customs duties. The passengers are watched closely by the officers. Their baggage may be searched if they look nervous or seem to have something to hide.

Sometimes, customs officers are warned that someone will be trying to **smuggle** drugs or other illegal goods into the country. They can use specially-trained dogs to help them find the smuggled goods, especially drugs. Drugs have even been found hidden inside coconuts and chocolates!

▼ Passengers have to pass through passport control before going through customs. The officer at passport control checks the expiration date, the photograph, and details in the passport.

Preventing the Spread of Disease

Customs officers also keep a lookout for people trying to smuggle animals, plants, or vegetables into a country. Diseases can be brought into a country by sick animals and plants that would infect other animals and people.

Some countries, like Britain, have strict controls on the import of animals. All animals going into that country have to be kept in **quarantine**. This means they are kept in isolation for a period of time until they are shown to be free of disease. The United States has rules that govern the movement of fruit and vegetables from one state to another. Many large airports have **health control** officers. Their job is to look out for passengers who may be suffering from infectious diseases.

▲ Customs officers test the bottom, top, and sides of a bag. Smugglers often conceal drugs or valuables under the lining or in a false bottom.

▶ Animals have to travel in special containers in the hold of an airliner. This is for their safety as well as for the safety of the passengers. When animals arrive in some countries they have to be kept in quarantine before their owners can collect them.

Beyond the Terminal

After showing their passports and going through the security checks, passengers wait in the departure lounge for their flight to be called. In many airports information about flights and flight delays is displayed on a large computer operated board, and sometimes on television screens around the departure area. At other airports, the airline staff also makes regular announcements on the loudspeaker system.

▲ The general public is never allowed on to runways at airports. Passengers may only cross the gate area when it is time for them to board a plane.

When the flight is called, passengers go to a numbered door or the **gate**, and show their boarding passes. They then walk along long enclosed ramps, that lead to the plane. Sometimes, passengers are taken by bus from the terminal to the plane, or simply walk across the gate area and up the plane steps.

Before Takeoff

In large airports, the ramps which stretch out from the terminal make it possible for several planes to use the terminal at the same time. It is while the planes are parked at the gates that engineers, fuel tanker drivers, and other workers prepare the planes for a flight. The gate area is connected to the runways by a number of concrete roads called **taxiways**.

Permission to use these taxiways and the runways can only be given by the controllers in the control tower, which is usually close to the terminal buildings. Beyond the runways, there is a **fuel depot**, which supplies the fuel used by the planes.

▼ Thousands of airport employees work at the gates or on runways at a major international airport. The employees have to carry special security passes.

The Runways

Large airports usually have at least two runways. These used to be built so that a pilot could expect to fly into the wind on takeoff. The wind helped to lift up the wings of the plane. Today, airliners are so powerful that this is no longer important. Instead, airport officials plan the runways so that planes can land and takeoff from the airport safely. Ideally, they do this over the sea or over land where there are very few buildings.

Keeping the Runways Clear

The engineers who design and build the runways make sure that the surface is smooth and safe for takeoffs and landings. They, and the airport workers who maintain the runways, are trained to look for weaknesses and cracks. These are repaired quickly when they are found so that the operation of the airport will not be interrupted.

▼ Runways at large airports usually run parallel to one another to avoid accidents. In this photograph taken from the air you can see the two runways above and below the terminal buildings. The diagonal lines that criss-cross the airport are taxiways.

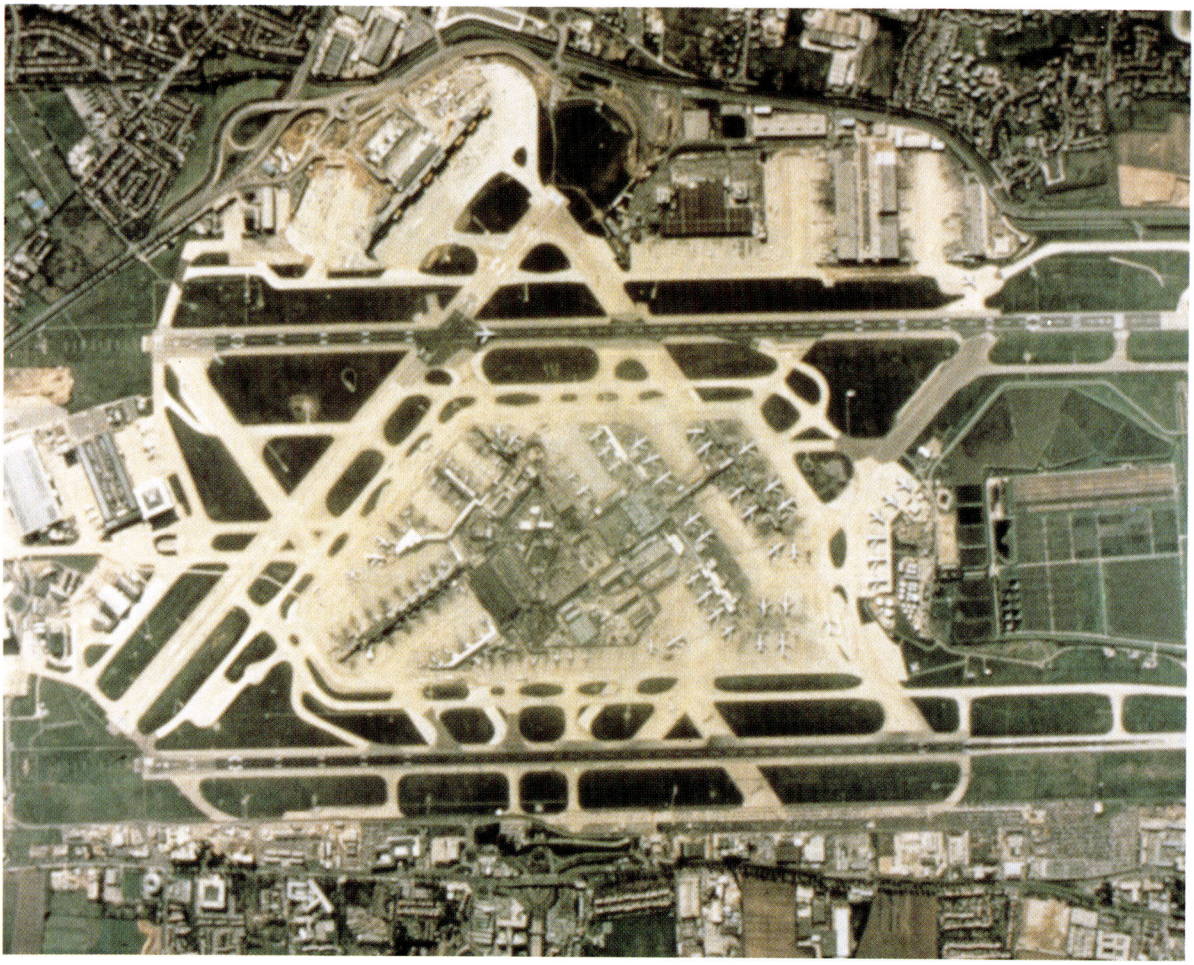

Maintenance workers sweep the runways clean of stones that could burst an airliner's tires. In the winter, they use machines to blow away the snow. They also use snowplows to clear thicker drifts. In desert airports, they have to sweep away the sand.

Birds are another problem. They like to gather in flocks at or near airports. This is dangerous for the birds and for the people on the planes because the birds can fly into the jet engines. The maintenance workers often use machines to scare the birds which make loud banging or wailing noises.

Guiding Lights

Runways have to be marked so that they can be seen clearly from the air, especially at night. This is why there are rows of lights on the approaches to, and on either side of, the runways. These lights can be seen by the pilot long before the plane touches down. Electrical engineers make sure that the runway lighting system is working properly and replace any broken lights.

▲ Airport staffmembers use a special vehicle to blow snow or sand off the runways so that the planes can take off.

▼ This car is towing a meter which measures the ability of aircraft to brake on the runway.

To the Rescue

The people working at an airport know that someday they may have to deal with an emergency. An airliner may crash or catch fire. A pilot may have to make an emergency landing. People may be injured or become sick on board an incoming plane.

Medical Help

Most large airports have a medical center with nurses and an airport doctor. The staff is always prepared for an emergency. Their vehicles and safety equipment are kept in good condition. They are always in radio contact with the control tower, and are alerted at once if they are needed. In a major crisis, the local police, fire department, and hospitals will also be alerted to the situation and called on for help.

▼ If the airline knows that someone will be needing medical help, they inform the medical center. A doctor and nurses can be waiting to help the patient as soon as the plane lands.

▲ Fire officers often use the shell of an old aircraft for practice. Most of the work done by the officers is training for the time when they are needed to put out a real fire.

The Fire Department

Most international airports have their own fire department and equipment. This equipment has to be made to fit the needs of an airport. The fire engines have especially long ladders because they have to be able to reach the tail of a jumbo jet which is over seventy feet high. The fire officers can be at the scene of a fire within a minute or two after the alarm. They expect to put out a fire in less than a minute. They use **chemical foam** instead of water. The foam smothers the burning fuel and keeps air from feeding the flames.

Fire officers know the risk they run if the fire spreads or if the fuel tanks blow up because of the heat of the fire. They have a very dangerous job.

The fire officers are also prepared to deal with other dangers as well. Some fire officers have **protective clothing** so that they can enter the burning airliner to rescue passengers. They wear air tanks and a mask to help them breathe in a smoke-filled cabin.

The Safety Record

Air travel is the safest form of transportation. Crashes are rare. Many airports have never had to deal with a major accident even though thousands of flights leave the airport every year. If an accident occurs, its cause is investigated fully to make sure it will not happen again.

Air Traffic Control

Air traffic controllers have a great deal of responsibility. They have to control the movements of many aircraft, on the ground or in the air, all at the same time. Controllers use their skills to help pilots land planes safely under all conditions, in good or bad weather, or in the dark. Controllers need to be alert at all times and think and act quickly when necessary.

Radio Contact

Air traffic controllers use radio to keep in touch with planes as they approach or leave an airport. They keep in close contact with the pilots at all times during landing or takeoff.

Ground controllers are responsible for the planes as soon as they are on the ground. They make sure that planes do not get in each other's way as they move along the taxiways and runways. The movements of planes on the ground are often shown in the control tower as lights on a huge map of the airport. The ground controllers use this map when telling pilots which taxiways to use. Only the ground controllers can give the pilots permission to take off.

When an aircraft is in the air, other controllers take over. These controllers use **radar** to pinpoint a plane's exact position in the sky. Radio waves are sent out, and when they meet the plane, they bounce back and show up on the radar screen as a small blob of light.

Each airliner is fitted with a **transponder**. This is a machine which sends details about the plane to the radar system. A computer which is part of the system changes the information into a code. This is shown on the screen. For example, if the code is BA 123 52 LL, this tells the air traffic controller the position of **B**ritish **A**irways Flight **123**. It also shows that the aircraft is flying at a height of **52,000** feet. The pilot is flying the plane to London, **LL** being the code for London.

◄ The control tower is always centrally placed so that the controllers have a good view across the entire airport.

Controlled Landings

When a plane approaches the airport, the pilot radios **approach control** for permission to land. If there are many planes waiting to land, the airliner will have to join the **stack**. This is a system where each plane flies around and around in a circle about 3,000 feet above and below the other airliners in the stack. As soon as the plane at the bottom lands, the air traffic controllers tell the pilots in the other planes in the stack to drop down to take the place of the plane below.

As each plane approaches the runway, the air traffic controllers help to guide the pilots until they have completed the landing.

▼ Permission for take-off and landing is given by staff in the control tower. At a busy airport they could be dealing with hundreds of flights an hour.

▼ The air traffic controllers have to guide all the aircraft on their screen safely on their way.

Checking the Aircraft

Engineers do some of the most important jobs at an airport. They make sure that the planes are safe to fly. They check the engines regularly, and make sure that everything works well. The engineers can take the plane apart, repair it, and put it back together again in perfect working order. They are trained to do these jobs well by the makers of the aircraft, or by the air force.

Service and Maintenance

Before a plane flies, it is given a **visual inspection** by the engineers. They look at it carefully to see if there are any obvious problems. They have been given information about any problems that the previous pilot may have noticed. The engineers must make sure that all the plane's instruments work and are accurate. They make sure the plane is safe to fly, or **airworthy**. They also check the tires.

▼ Many of the routine repair and cleaning jobs on an airliner can be done while it is standing at the gate.

▶ X-ray machines are used to check to see if there are any cracks in the metal of the plane.

▼ These engineers are servicing an airliner in the hanger. They strip down the engines and replace any parts that are broken or worn out.

A careful record of the number of hours flown by each plane is kept. After 1,000 hours' flying time, the engineers take the plane into a **hangar** for one-day service. A hanger is a huge garage for planes. The engineers check the plane's engines, tires, brakes, lights, and instruments.

After several thousand hours' flying time, the engineers do a complete **overhaul** on the plane. They examine the metal frame of the airliner closely with X-ray machines. They check to see if there are any cracks. They take out the instruments from the flight deck and test each one. New instruments are put in if there is any sign of wear.

The engineers take the engines apart in order to test the different parts and replace any that are faulty. Each engine is tested until it is working perfectly. Every part of the plane is tested and repaired or replaced in the same way. On some airlines, even the seats inside the passenger cabin are replaced.

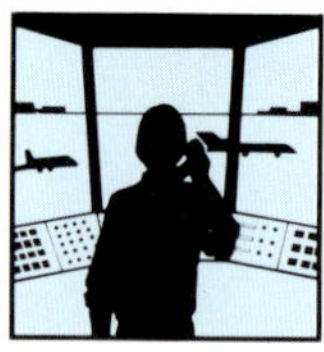

Taking on Fuel

▼ The flight engineer has to keep a constant check on the amount of fuel remaining during a flight. He has to make sure that there is enough to get the plane to its destination.

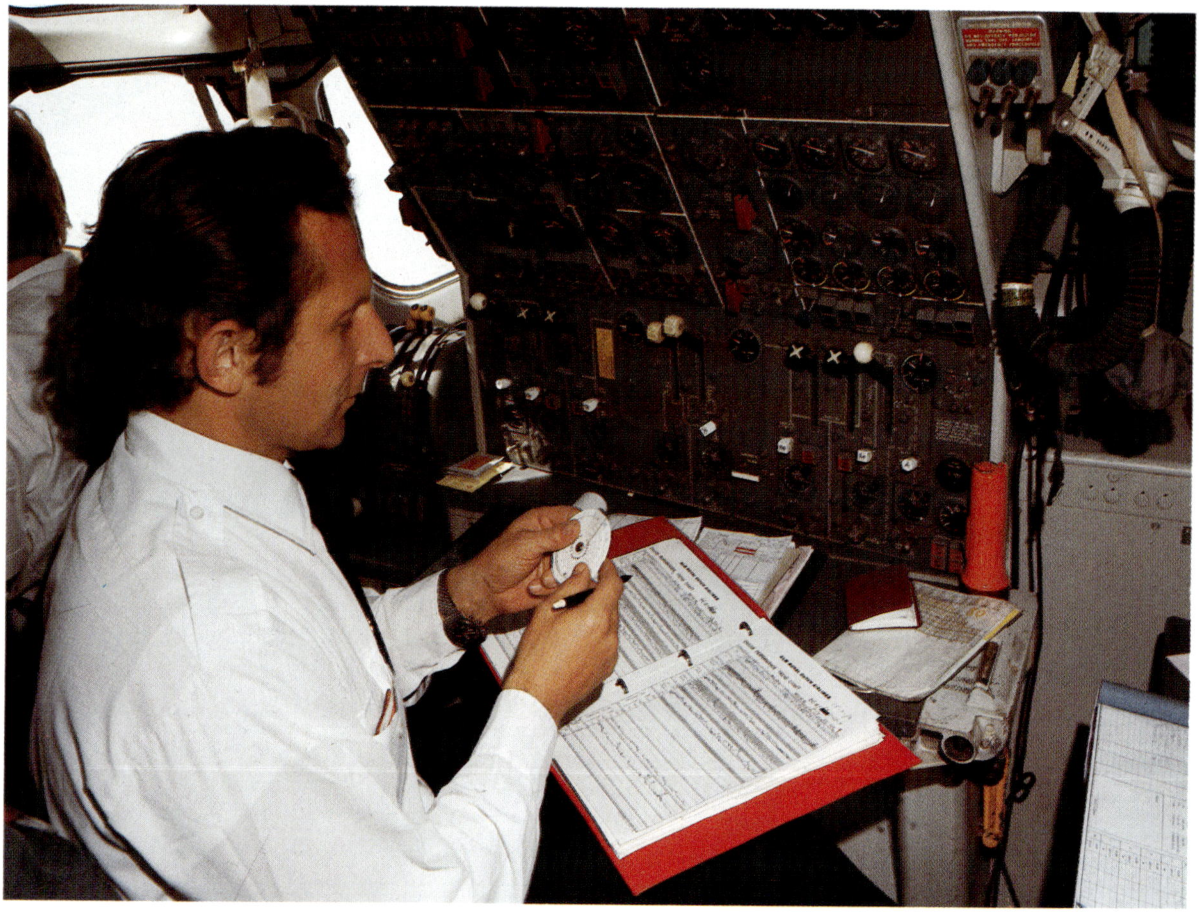

Airliners burn up huge amounts of **aviation fuel**. Some use as much as 2,000 gallons an hour. This is why the fuel tanks of a jumbo jet are designed to hold 25,000 gallons of fuel. The equivalent amount of gasoline would keep a family car going for one hundred years!

Refueling

Many workers are employed to bring fuel to the planes as they stand at the gates outside the terminal. The tanker drivers know that a plane must be filled up quickly between flights to prevent a delay to passengers or cargo. They refill the tanks with aviation fuel. Each driver can bring between 5,000 and 10,000 gallons of fuel to the plane in a single tanker. High-speed pumps push the fuel through fuel lines into the plane. Even so, it may take up to twenty minutes to fill up a jumbo jet.

During the Flight

Huge quantities of fuel are very heavy for a plane to carry. A jumbo jet may be carrying over fifty tons of fuel at takeoff.

Extra weight slows down the plane and may mean that fewer passengers can be carried. This is why the captain of a plane has to figure out exactly how much fuel the plane will need on the journey. It will depend partly on the size of the plane and the combined weight of passengers, cargo, and fuel. It will also depend on the strength of the winds and the direction from which they are blowing.

Weather forecasts inform the captain of the winds the plane will face on the journey. If the plane is flying with the wind, it will use less fuel. If it is flying against the wind, the plane will use more. When the captain has figured out how much fuel is needed, he or she gives this information to the tanker drivers. They fill up the plane's tanks with that amount, together with a small amount in reserve in case of an emergency.

Storing Fuel

After filling up a plane the airport tanker drivers collect more fuel from the fuel depot on the edge of the airport. At some airports, however, the fuel is piped directly from the depot to the area outside the terminal. From there it can then be pumped directly into the airliner's fuel tanks. This method is safer and lessens the fire risk.

► Aviation fuel is carried in tankers from the main depot, or storage area, to the plane waiting at the gate. The fuel is then pumped on board the aircraft.

The Flight Crew

While the passengers are checking in, the flight crew of the airliner prepares for takeoff. The captain and the first officer study the **flight plan**. This is the timetable showing the route to be taken by the plane, its speed, the height at which it will fly, and the time at which it is expected to arrive. The plan is prepared by the captain with the help of experts in the airline's **operations and control room**.

Before the flight, the flight crew looks at the weather reports and finds out how many passengers and how much cargo the plane will be carrying. The captain then calculates the amount of fuel that is needed.

Flying the Plane

First, the crew goes on board, and makes a **pre-flight check** to see that all the instruments are working properly. The instruments give the flight crew the information that is needed to fly the plane. They show how high the plane is flying, its speed, direction, how much fuel is left, and whether the engines are working properly.

The captain sits in the left-hand seat in front of the controls on the **flight deck**. The first officer, or **copilot**, sits in front of a second set of controls on the right. On large airliners, there is usually a flight engineer who sits behind the captain and gives technical support. The captain is in complete charge of the airliner. There may be as many as 500 passengers on board, and a jumbo jet is worth many millions of dollars. It is important for him or her to be extremely responsible and careful.

◀ The captain is being briefed on the type of weather he will meet during the flight.

▲ The flight deck of an airliner is full of instruments. This vast array of dials, knobs, and switches enables the flight crew to fly the airliner to its destination in safety. Everything must be checked before takeoff.

▼ Most pilots learn how to fly a new type of plane by sitting at the controls of a flight simulator like this one.

A Skilled Job

Flying an airliner is a highly skilled job. Some airline pilots first learn to fly in their country's air force. Others join the airline straight out of college. All pilots have to be healthy and fit, and they must have regular medical checkups as long as they are actively flying.

Even when pilots have qualified, they have to continue their training because they must be prepared for anything that may happen. They train on a **flight simulator**, a machine which looks like the real flight deck of an airliner. Each time the pilot touches the controls of the simulator, a computer is programmed to make the machine move like an airliner. It is possible to imitate bad weather and emergency situations, such as engine failure. Pilots can train like this without the risk of an actual accident.

On the Plane

When passengers board a plane, they are greeted by the members of the cabin crew. These are the flight attendants, whose job it is to look after the passengers during the flight. The flight attendants have been trained to show the passengers to their seats and answer their questions, and they try to solve any problems the passengers may put to them. The flight attendants also have to make sure that all the passengers' hand luggage is safely stored away under the seats or in the overhead lockers.

Safety First

Safety is an important part of the attendants' duties. The attendants make sure that all passengers put on their safety belts before takeoff and landing. They demonstrate how to put on **lifejackets** and point out the emergency exits. All the members of the cabin crew are trained to operate and use the emergency chutes. These are special tubes or slides that the passengers and crew can use to escape from the plane after a crash.

The crew are all fully trained to cope with anything that may happen. They know how to fight a fire if it breaks out on board the plane while it is in flight. They are also trained in **first aid** in case of accident or illness during the flight.

◄ The flight attendants tell the passengers what to do in case of emergency. At the start of the flights, they show the passengers how to operate life jackets and how to use oxygen masks.

▲ It is the job of the cabin crew to see that passengers have a comfortable flight. They may have to reassure first-time travelers or look after small children. Here, the flight attendants are preparing meals in the galley, or kitchen, of the airliner.

▼ Passengers on most flights are given something to eat and drink on board.

Serving Food

The members of the cabin crew also serve meals and drinks to the passengers. They do not cook the food on the plane. Instead, the meals are cooked and prepared in advance. Trucks take the food to the plane just before it leaves. The food is heated in the galley of the plane in a microwave oven during the flight.

To help in their training, the attendants learn their duties on the ground in a full-size model of a passenger cabin.

A Rewarding Job

Working as a member of the cabin crew is a hard but interesting job. Crew members work long hours, but many of them travel all over the world. They may be away from home for several days at a time if they are on an international flight. Many members of the cabin crew are hired because they can speak more than one language.

Takeoff

All the fuel needed for the flight is on board, the baggage and cargo are loaded, and the meals for the flight are in the galley. All the service vehicles that have been loading these items onto the plane have moved away from the airliner. The flight attendants count the passengers to make sure that the numbers agree with those on the check-in list.

Shortly before takeoff, a powerful tractor, called an **air tug**, pulls the airliner away from the gate. Inside the cabin, smokers must put out their cigarettes and all passengers must fasten their seat belts. The cabin crew makes sure that this is done.

▼ An air tug tows a Boeing 747 into position so that the pilot can use the airliner's engines to taxi onto the runway.

Final Checks

The members of the flight crew make their final check. When they are ready, they radio the control tower. They ask for permission to start the engines. When this is given, engineers outside the plane start it with a power source on wheels, known as a **mobile generator**.

The pilot moves the plane slowly down the taxiway leading to the end of the runway. There, the plane has to wait before the ground control gives it permission to take off. There is a short pause while the flight crew checks their engines and instruments for the last time before take-off. The control tower then gives the go-ahead, and the engines are switched on to full power.

The flight crew release the airliner's brakes. The plane starts to move. It goes faster and faster. It may cover a distance of over two miles before it is traveling fast enough to leave the ground. The pilot touches the controls, the wings lift the plane off the runway, and it climbs steeply into the sky.

▲ The minute the plane leaves the runway, the pilot puts it into a steep climb in order to avoid any tall buildings and to cause the least noise disturbance to people living near the airport.

The Flight

During the flight the members of the crew keep in touch with the ground by radio. Once the course of the flight has been set, they can leave the plane in the hands of the **automatic pilot**. This is the machine which automatically alters the direction of the airliner so that it will stay on course without assistance from the pilot. The flight crew keep in touch with the air traffic controllers in charge of the airspace through which they are traveling. English is used throughout the world as the language of the controllers.

When the airliner is close to its destination, the flight crew radios approach control in the airport control tower. They are given permission to land, and a radar operator guides them in.

▲ From the moment that a plane approaches an airport until the moment that the plane lands, the pilot is in constant radio contact with air traffic control.

Flying Cargo

Most airports do a lot of business with firms which send cargo by air instead of by rail, sea, or road. About half the world's air cargo travels in the hold of passenger airliners. The other half travels in special cargo planes which have their own terminal at an airport.

The cargo terminal is usually situated on the edge of the airport. It can easily be reached by truck drivers bringing cargo to the terminal on the roads leading to the airport.

Sorting Cargo

The cargo is stored in warehouses at the cargo terminal before and after a flight. The cargo terminal workers label the cargo and use computers to calculate the cost of transportation. They also calculate how much cargo can be loaded into each plane.

The goods are then sorted for the different flights. They have to be checked against the cargo manifest or list of goods traveling on a particular flight. All cargo is also checked by the customs officers. Some goods are packed into large metal containers called "igloos", which are specially shaped to fit into the space inside the body of the airliner. Other goods are placed on flat trays usually made of wood.

▼ When animals, whether giraffes or chickens, are sent by air, the greatest care is taken to ensure that they travel safely. The advantage of sending animals by air is that they will arrive at their destination much quicker than by sea or land.

► Cargo handlers use a special machine to lift cargo on a platform until it is level with the floor of the hold of the airliner. The handlers then load the cargo into the hold so that the weight is spread evenly.

Why Use a Plane?

Sending cargo by plane is expensive. It is only worthwhile if the goods are likely to spoil quickly, such as fresh fruit and vegetables, or if they have a high value. Goods are also sent by air if they are needed urgently, such as letters, medical supplies, newspapers, and vital parts for engines or machines.

Some types of cargo have to be guarded by security officers. Valuable cargo like this may include large amounts of money, precious stones, and even gold bars.

Loading cargo

The cargo handlers have to move cargo of all shapes and sizes. There can be anything from live monkeys and fresh fruit to cars and furniture. In larger airports, the cargo handlers use forklift trucks, small cranes, or conveyor belts to move goods into the cargo hold of the plane. Engineers open the tail or the nose of the plane to make it easier to load. The cargo hold is fitted with rails and rollers. These are used by the cargo handlers to slide the containers and trays into the hold.

The Future

No one knows what it will be like to work at an airport in the future. It is possible that huge jumbo jets flying faster than Concorde may carry thousands of passengers in one plane from Sydney to New York or London. If this happened, then air travel would be a lot less expensive than it is right now.

Fuel

Such flights would only be possible if a better and cheaper fuel for aircraft engines was found. Some people fear that airports will be closed down because the world's supplies of oil seem to be running out. It is possible to make aviation fuel from coal, but at the moment this costs too much.

▼ Airports of the future could be very different from airports today. Many things may have changed and the jobs people do may be different too.

44

▲ Some people think the airports of the future will be seadromes. They could be built on long platforms reaching out into the sea. Airports like this would have many advantages. There would be no hills or buildings to get in the way when airliners landed. Only a very few people would be bothered by the noise.

Short and Long Runways

Planes of the future may need much less fuel than they do now. They may need short runways, too. If this happened, then the need for large airports would no longer exist. Small airliners could take off from the roofs of buildings in the city centers just like helicopters do today.

However, if airliners were designed to travel faster, they would need very long runways. If this were to happen, the airports would have to be moved farther away from the cities. They could be built over the sea where there is plenty of space.

New Airports

It is possible that the airports of the future will be run more and more by computers and automatic machines. These could do many of the jobs which are currently done by people. Automatic ticket machines might take the place of the staff at the check-in desk. Computers could be programmed to answer passengers' questions in any language. Automatic machines would serve hot food and drinks, and there might even be automatic security checks. Even the airliners could be staffed by robots and automatic pilots. Whatever the future brings, airports will always be exciting and busy places to work.

Glossary

administrator: a person who is in charge of the running of a big organization such as an airport.

airline: a company which provides flights from place to place.

airliner: a large aircraft owned by an airline which carries passengers and cargo.

airmail: letters or parcels which are carried by plane.

airport authority: the organization which runs an airport.

airspace: the area of sky above a particular country.

air traffic controller: an official, usually based at an airport, who controls the movement of aircraft in the air or on the ground.

air tug: a powerful vehicle used to pull or push airliners into position on the ground at an airport.

airworthy: describes a plane which is safe to fly.

approach control: the group of people who are in charge of plane movements near an airport.

automatic pilot: a machine or process which keeps an aircraft flying on a fixed course by itself.

aviation fuel: the type of fuel which is burned by jet engines.

baggage train: a long line of wagons which carry baggage.

boarding pass: a card issued to a passenger enabling him or her to board an aircraft.

cargo: the goods carried by a ship or plane.

cargo hold: the space in a ship or on an aircraft used for carrying goods.

carousel: a machinelike merry-go-round on which baggage is put in an airport for passengers to claim their luggage after a flight.

check in: to report at an airport with a ticket and baggage before a flight.

chemical foam: a mixture of froth and bubbles produced by chemicals. It smothers flames and prevents air from getting to them.

control tower: the tall building at an airport where all the orders are given to planes at or near the airport.

conveyor belt: a continuous moving track which is used to carry goods from one place to another.

copilot: the pilot who assists the captain of an aircraft.

customs: the place where goods or baggage are checked by government officers. These officers make sure that the correct taxes are paid on goods entering or leaving the country. They also make sure that no forbidden goods or animals are being carried. Customs officers also check passengers' passports.

domestic flight: a flight which takes place entirely inside a country.

duty free: describes goods from foreign countries on which no tax has been charged.

first aid: immediate help given to someone who is sick or injured.

flight deck: the place from which the pilot and other members of the flight crew operate the airliner.

flight plan: the details of the route to be taken by an aircraft and how long the flight will take.

flight simulator: a machine which imitates the movements of an airliner in flight.

fuel depot: a storage place for fuel.

gate: the door through which passengers leave the terminal building in order to board a plane.

ground controller: the person in the airport control tower who controls the movements of aircraft on the ground.

hangar: a large building where planes are kept or are taken to be repaired. Cargo is also stored in a hangar.

health control: the group of officials which enforces governmental laws concerning public health.

immigration control: a government department which controls the entry of people into a country.

jumbo jet: a huge airliner. The phrase is most often used to describe the Boeing 747 airliner.

lifejacket: a type of sleeveless jacket which fills up with air and keeps a person's head above water in order to prevent drowning.

metal detector: a machine or device which can find objects made of metal in a passenger's clothes or baggage.

mobile generator: an electric generator mounted on a vehicle. It is used at an airport to start the engines of an airliner.

operations and control room: the room from which an airline organizes the movements of its airliners around the world.

overhaul: to give an engine, machine, or vehicle a thorough checkup and service.

passport: a small book given to someone by a country's government to say that he or she is from that country and may travel abroad.

pre-flight check: the check made by the members of the flight crew of an airliner before takeoff.

protective clothing: clothes which protect people, such as firefighters, against flames, and smoke.

quarantine: the place where, or the period of time when, people or animals are kept apart from each other in order to prevent the spread of a disease.

radar: a method of using radio beams to detect the position of objects at a distance, such as aircraft or ships.

security officer: an official employed at an airport to ensure the safety of the airport workers and passengers.

shuttle flight: a regular, daily air service used by passengers who do not need to book a ticket in advance.

smuggle: to secretly carry something, such as illegal drugs, into another country.

stack: a line of aircraft at an airport waiting to land. Planes are stacked by flying around at different heights above and below each other.

taxiway: a wide concrete pathway which connects the runway and the gate areas.

terminal: a building at an airport where passengers or cargo arrive, or from which they depart.

transponder: an electronic device attached to an airliner which allows details of the flight to be picked up by radar.

visa: a document which gives a person permission to enter a foreign country for a specific purpose or period of time.

visual inspection: a careful physical check made by someone without the aid of instruments or machines.

X-ray machine: a device used at airports to check the contents of passengers' baggage.

Index